Applying the Love of Christ
to Dating Relationships

Study Guide

ROB EAGAR

GRACE
PRESS

The Power of Passion
Applying the Love of Christ to Dating Relationships
Study Guide
published by Grace Press

Copyright © 2004 by Rob Eagar

For more information, please contact:
Grace Press Publishing
3625 Chartwell Dr.
Suwanee, GA 30024
1-800-267-2045
www.powerofpassion.com

Unless otherwise noted, all Scripture quotations in this book are taken from the NEW AMERICAN STANDARD BIBLE®, Copyright © 1960, 1962, 1963, 1968, 1971, 1972, 1973, 1977, 1995 by The Lockman Foundation. Used by permission.

Scripture quotations marked (NLT) are taken from the *Holy Bible,* New Living Translation, copyright © 1996. Used by permission of Tyndale House Publishers, Inc., Wheaton, Illinois 60189. All rights reserved.

All italics used in Scripture quotations are added by the author.

All rights reserved. Making and distributing copies of the Power of Passion DVD Study Guide material is prohibited. No part of this publication may be reproduced, stored in a retrieval system, or transmitted, in any form or by any means, electronic–mechanical, photocopying, recording, or any other–except for brief quotations in printed reviews or articles, without the prior written permission of the publisher.

ISBN 0-9717486-1-6

Printed in the United States of America

This Study Guide is a companion to
The Power of Passion
Applying the Love of Christ to Dating Relationships
Video DVD Study.
To for more information, visit: www.powerofpassion.com

How to Use this Study Guide with a Small Group

This Study Guide contains eight sessions that accompany The Power of Passion DVD Video Study. We recommend that each person have a Study Guide, which will enable them to follow along with Rob Eagar's presentations. *Making and distributing copies of the Power of Passion DVD Study Guide material is prohibited.* This Study Guide contains:

- a group kickoff question
- an introduction of each session topic
- a listing of the Bible verses mentioned
- key fill-in-the-blank statements
- personal questions to consider
- and small group discussion questions

To conduct an 8-session group study, begin with the kickoff question, read the introduction, then play the DVD and follow along in the Study Guide. Each video session runs approximately 20 – 35 minutes. After watching the video segment, use the discussion questions at the end of each session to talk about the lesson in more detail.

How to Use this Study Guide at a Conference

At a live Power of Passion Conference, Rob Eagar gives four presentations. This Study Guide has been modified into eight sections and two sections cover each of Rob's presentations. Use this booklet to take notes, read the Bible verses mentioned, complete the key fill-in-the-blank statements, and answer the personal questions at the end of each session.

About the Author

Rob Eagar is the author of *The Power of Passion – Applying the Love of Christ to Dating Relationships*. He holds a Bachelors Degree in Marketing from *Auburn University* and a Doctorate in Dating from the "School of Hard Knocks."

Rob has helped thousands of singles revolutionize their dating and spiritual lives. His ministry has been featured on the *CBS Early Show, CNN Radio,* and *Christian Single Magazine.* Rob has inspired singles and young adults at churches across America, including *Saddleback Church, McLean Bible Church, and Willow Creek Community Church.*

Rob resides in Atlanta, Georgia with his wife, Ashley, where they attend *North Point Community Church.* When Rob isn't speaking or writing, he enjoys hiking, tennis, and playing his drums as loud as possible. However, Ashley prefers that he join her to quietly paint, work in their garden, or watch Jane Austen movies.

Contents

Session #1 – The Power of Passion
Discovering the Longing of Your Heart

Kickoff Question:

Ask each group member to tell who their favorite TV or movie couple is and why.

Video Introduction:

Each one of us was created with a heart that desperately needs love. Yet, our society claims that the best way to fulfill our hungry hearts is through romantic passion. In other words, find that perfect emotional or sexual relationship, then you will find your "happily ever after." Is this popular notion really true? In this session, Rob Eagar shares how his personal pursuit of romance led him to a life-changing realization.

Video Notes:

Our society says the best way to satisfy your heart is through

_____ _____.

A man wants to be loved as a _____. A woman feels loved

when the hero _____ her.

Why is relational heartache common among Christians? We try to fulfill our hearts with something that cannot _____.

The Problem with Romantic Passion:

Human love is like _____.

Romantic Passion is always _____.

Romantic Passion is also always _____.

What we all want is to be unconditionally _____.

How does God want you to respond to what you heard today?

_____

_____

_____

_____

_____

For further study on the topics in this session, read Chapter 1
in Rob's book, *The Power of Passion.*

Session #1
Small Group Discussion Questions

1) Discuss how movies, television, or music has shaped your ideas about romance. Give specific examples.

2) What is the common problem between a chocolate sugar high and a romantic, emotional high?

3) Since romantic passion is temporary, list some ways that couples perform for each other early in their relationship which later stop.

4) In this video lesson, Rob mentioned how prayer and reading the Bible helped him recover from relational pain. Two of his favorite verses are Isaiah 41:10 and John 14:27. Read these verses aloud and discuss how God's word offers healing during heartache or trying times. Suggest any other verses that have personally encouraged you.

Session #2 – The Power of Passion
Discovering Real Passion

Kickoff Question:

Ask each group member to express what ideas come to mind when he or she hears the word "passion"?

Video Introduction:

In the previous lesson, Rob shared his tragic story and explained why human love is like chocolate. Relationships can make you feel good, but romantic passion is always temporary and performance-based. The emotional high never lasts. In this lesson, Rob explains how a new type of passion is waiting to satisfy your heart.

Video Notes:

The 3 Elements of Real Passion:

Hebrews 12:2 – Fix your eyes upon Jesus, the author and perfecter of our faith, who for the joy set before Him, endured the cross, despised the shame, and sat down at the right hand of the throne of God.

Element #1: Real Passion loves me _____.

    1 John 4:19 – We love, because He first loved us.

    Titus 3:4-5 – But when the kindness of God our Savior and His love for mankind appeared, He saved us, not on the basis of deeds which we have done in righteousness, but according to His mercy.

Element #2: Real Passion loves me _____.

    Luke 12:6-7 – What is the price of five sparrows? A couple of pennies? Yet God does not forget a single one of them. And the very hairs on your head are all numbered. So do not be afraid; you are more valuable to Him than a whole flock of sparrows.

Element #3: Real Passion loves me _____.

    Ephesians 5:2 – And walk in love, just as Christ also loved you and gave Himself up for us, an offering and a sacrifice to God.

    2 Corinthians 5:21 – God made Jesus who knew no sin, to become sin our behalf, that we might become the righteousness of God in Him.

Jesus Christ loves me: _____, _____,

and _____.

Questions to consider:

1. Do I base my self-esteem on whether or not I have a boyfriend or girlfriend?

2. Do I feel like I have to get married someday in order to be happy?

3. Do I really believe that Jesus Christ loves me unconditionally, even when I sin?

How does God want you to respond to what you heard today?

_____

_____

_____

_____

_____

For further study on the topics in this session, read Chapter 1
in Rob's book, *The Power of Passion*.

Session #2
Small Group Discussion Questions

1) What substitutes does Satan offer to pull us away from the real passion of Jesus Christ?

2) In Titus 3:5, the Apostle Paul wrote, "He (Jesus) saved us, not on the basis on deeds which we have done in righteousness, but according to His mercy." Why is this statement so important?

3) Have each group member share one experience from their life where they witnessed sacrificial love.

4) Discuss which of the three elements of real passion mean the most to you. Why are all three elements important?

Session #3 – Choose Your Passion
Determining the Best Person to Date

Kickoff Question:

Find out which group member has the funniest blind date story.

Video Introduction:

The quality of a dating relationship is determined by the quality of the two people involved. Therefore, one of the toughest decisions you face as a single adult is choosing whom you date. A poor choice could have lasting consequences, or a wise decision could reap lifelong benefits. In this session, Rob reveals how the love of Jesus Christ offers practical and spiritual insight into this dating dilemma.

Video Notes:

Just because someone is _____ or professes to be a

_____ does not make them a good marriage partner.

Write down four key qualities that you desire in a husband or wife.

- •   •

- •   •

Pursue someone who attracts you _____ but is willing to love you _____.

What is your favorite flavor of ice cream? _____

As a Christian, you can trust your _____.

> Ezekiel 36:26 – I will give you a new heart and put a new spirit in you.

> Ephesians 3:17 – Christ may dwell in your hearts through faith...

In Ephesians 5, God calls men to _____ a relationship.

How does God want you to respond to what you heard today?

_____

_____

_____

_____

_____

For further study on the topics in this session, read Chapter 4
in Rob's book, *The Power of Passion*.

Session #3
Small Group Discussion Questions

1) Why does someone who claims to be a Christian not necessarily mean that he or she would make a good dating partner?

2) Read Luke 12:6–7 and Psalms 139:17–18, then discuss how these verses reveal Christ's specific attraction towards us.

3) Discuss why we are often afraid to trust our heart or inner preferences.

4) Read Ephesians 5:23, 25. According to these verses, why does God want men to take the initiative in a dating relationship?

Session #4 – Choose Your Passion
Learning to Discern Character

Kickoff Question:

Have each group member reveal something they learned about love from their first boyfriend or girlfriend.

Video Introduction:

In the previous lesson, Rob revealed how pursuing a person who specifically attracts you illustrates the unique fascination that Jesus Christ feels for you. However, outward qualities alone cannot keep a relationship together. Couples need more than just an outward attraction to stay together. In this session, Rob explains the key ingredient that is essential to building a passionate relationship.

Video Notes:

Specific Attraction can bring two people together, but only

_____ can keep them together.

Ephesians 5:25 – Husbands, love your wives, just as Christ loved the church and gave Himself up for her.

Romans 5:8 – God showed his great love for us by sending Christ to die for us while we were still sinners.

The definition of Marriage is a _____ to an

_____ person for their _____ good.

7 Ways to Examine the Character of Your Date:
1. Does my date allow our relationship to progress naturally?
2. Does my date dress in a way that doesn't tempt the opposite sex to lust?
3. Is my date able to forgive people when they make mistakes or act rudely?
4. Is my date overly self-conscious about what people think of him or her?
5. Can my date abstain from sex - even if other people encourage the issue?
6. Does my date talk too much about himself, or ask questions about me?
7. Does my date show generosity with time and money to those in need?

Character can only be determined over _____.

John 15:5 – I am the vine, you are the branches; he who abides in Me and I in him will bear much fruit (love, joy, peace, patience, etc.); for apart from Me you can do nothing.

1 Corinthians 2:16 – Who can know what the Lord is thinking? We can understand, for we have the mind of Christ.

Do not ask Jesus to give you more patience. Instead, ask Him to give

you _____ patience.

Questions to consider:

1. Are you willing to pursue a passionate romance than settle for companionship or security?

2. Will you yield to Christ and love someone else sacrificially?

3. If you're dating, is sacrificial love absent in your relationship or one-sided?

How does God want you to respond to what you heard today?

_____

_____

_____

_____

_____

For further study on the topics in this session, read Chapters 4 and 9 in Rob's book, *The Power of Passion*.

Session #4
Small Group Discussion Questions

1) What is the "true" definition of marriage? How does this compare to the world's definition of marriage?

2) Discuss why it is impossible for people to love sacrificially. Why is Jesus Christ our only source of hope?

3) Read 1 John 4:7–10, and reflect on the sacrificial love that Jesus offered you. Then, come up with three ways that sacrificial love could be exhibited in a dating relationship.

4) Why is time essential to determining another person's character?

Session #5 – The Bond of Passion
Appreciating Sexual Desire

Kickoff Question:

Find out which group member has the funniest first kiss story.

Video Introduction:

Many singles fall into a pattern of dating that involves physical affection followed by heartache. This cycle happens when they date someone, go overboard sensually, spoil their relationship, and feel broken inside after they separate. Yet, God says sex is supposed to be for our good. If so, then why do so many people crave or misuse it? In this session, Rob explains the "why" behind the "what" concerning the most controversial subject in dating.

Video Notes:

Why can Sex Feel so Good?

1. God primarily created sex to help you comprehend the

_____ that He feels for you.

Isaiah 62:3-4 – You will be a crown of beauty in the hand of the Lord. For the Lord delights in you!

Ephesians 5:25-27 – (Christ) gave Himself up for her; that He might sanctify her, having cleansed her by the washing of water with the word, that He might present to Himself the Church in all her glory, having no spot or wrinkle or such thing; that she should be holy and blameless.

If we use sex outside of marriage, then we destroy the _____

that God intended it to be.

2. You were made to be _____ and accepted.

Why can Sex Hurt so Bad?

1 Corinthians 6:13-18 – ...the body is not for immorality, but for the Lord, and the Lord is for the body...Do you not know that your bodies are members of Christ? Shall I then take away the members of Christ and make them members with a harlot? No! Don't you know that if a man joins himself to a prostitute, he becomes one body with her? For the Scriptures say, "The two are united into one." But the person who is joined to the Lord becomes one spirit with Him. Run away from sexual sin! No other sin so clearly affects the body as this one. For sexual immorality is a sin against your own body. (NLT)

Sex is a physical act that _____ the bodies and

souls of two people together.

The Hidden Damage from Sexual Immorality:

1. Loss of the capacity to _____ intimacy for another person.

2. Contraction of painful or deadly transmitted _____.

3. Carrying a heavy, emotional _____ of guilt and shame.

How does God want you to respond to what you heard today?

_____

_____

_____

_____

_____

For further study on the topics in this session, read Chapter 7
in Rob's book, *The Power of Passion*.

Session #5
Small Group Discussion Questions

1) List three lies that our media industry promotes about sex.

2) Read 1 Corinthians 6:18. Based on this verse and Rob's talk, in what ways does sex outside of marriage cause physical and emotional consequences?

3) Why does sexual activity immediately change the atmosphere of a relationship?

4) Discuss how it feels to realize that we are naked and totally accepted before God.

Session #6 – The Bond of Passion
Resisting Sexual Temptation

Kickoff Question:

Talk about some of the popular diet fads that you have tried and consider why they are so difficult to maintain.

Video Introduction:

How do you stay pure in a society that bombards you with sexual images, references, and innuendos? Is it possible to enjoy a passionate relationship without going too far sexually? How do you stand firm when everyone else is doing it? In this session, Rob reveals the most overlooked secret to victory over sexual temptation.

Video Notes:

Living by rules alone will encourage sin to _____ you.

> Romans 7:7-8 – I would not have come to know sin except through the Law; for I would not have known about coveting if the Law hadn't said, "You shall not covet." But sin, taking opportunity through the Law, produced in me coveting of every kind; apart from the Law – sin is dead.

Galatians 3:24-25 - Therefore the Law has become our tutor to lead us to Christ, that we may be justified by faith. But now that faith has come, we are no longer under a tutor.

2 Corinthians 5:14 - For the love of Christ controls us...

How do you resist temptation? Let _____ fight the battle

for you.

2 Corinthians 12:9 - And He said to me, "My grace is sufficient for you, for power is perfected in weakness." Most gladly, therefore, I will rather boast about my weaknesses, that the power of Christ may dwell in me.

Galatians 5:16, 24 - ...walk by the Spirit, and you will not carry out the lust of the flesh...Now those who belong to Christ have crucified the flesh with its passions and desires.

Colossians 1:11 - ...strengthened with His glorious power so that you will have all the patience and endurance you need... (NLT)

Healing Your Heart from a Sexual Mistake:

1. _____ with God that you misused His gift of sex.

2. _____ yourself - knowing God has forgiven you.

3. Let you heart _____ before you date again.

Questions to consider:

Ladies:
1. Would you be willing to depend on Christ for the power to say "no" when your boyfriend pushes you for sex?

2. Would you be willing to sacrifice being in vogue and avoid deliberately wearing clothes that makes men lust?

Men:
1. Would you be willing to sacrifice your immediate sexual desires and not push your girlfriend for sex?

2. Would you be willing to protect your relationships with women by guarding your mind from porn and trashy movies?

How does God want you to respond to what you heard today?

_____

_____

_____

_____

_____

For further study on the topics in this session, read Chapter 8 in Rob's book, *The Power of Passion.*

Session #6
Small Group Discussion Questions

1) Discuss why fighting sexual temptation through your own willpower leads to defeat.

2) What are some of practical ways that Christ can help disarm temptation for you?

3) Read Ephesians 4:17–24. According to these verses, how does sinful behavior originate? What is your defense against sexual immorality?

4) Discuss the benefits of maintaining sexual purity.

Session #7 – Where's the Passion?
Recognizing God's Role in Your Social Life

Kickoff Question:

If you could ask God one question about dating, what would it be?

Video Introduction:

One of the most frustrating questions single adults face is, "Why am I still single?" The pressure to get married from well-meaning friends or your biological clock can create a devastating level of anxiety. This stress can also cause a Christian to wonder if God really cares about his or her dating life. In this session, Rob explores whether or not God is involved in our relationships.

Video Notes:

Marriage Myth #1:

Marriage will make you _____.

Marriage Myth #2:

If you're single, then something must be _____ with you.

Is God to blame for singleness or social suffering? _____
(Job 1:8-19; Luke 22:31-32)

True love cannot exist without a _____ _____.

The quality of your social life is based on the _____ you make.

> Romans 8:31-39 – ...If God is for us, who is against us?...Who shall separate us from the love of Christ? Shall tribulation, or distress, or persecution?...In all these things we overwhelmingly conquer through Him who loved us. For I am convinced that nothing...shall be able to separate us from the love of God, which is in Christ Jesus our Lord.

What Part does God Play in Your Social Life?

1. God promises to bring _____ across your _____.

> Ephesians 2:10 – For we are His workmanship, created in Christ Jesus for good works, which God prepared beforehand that we should walk in them.

2. God promises to create _____ within you to _____

those He brings across your path.

> Philippians 2:13 – For it is God who is at work in you, to will and to work for His good pleasure.

God does not intend to direct your love life through a bunch of

extraordinary _____.

God's will for your social life is to _____ your

character into a loving kind of person.

> Colossians 3:10,12 ...put on the new self who is being renewed to a true knowledge according the image of the One who created you...put on a heart of compassion, kindness, humility, gentleness, and patience.

How does God want you to respond to what you heard today?

_____

_____

_____

_____

_____

For further study on the topics in this session, read Chapter 3
in Rob's book, *The Power of Passion*.

Session #7
Small Group Discussion Questions

1) Beside the two marriage myths that Rob described, what other false expectations do many people harbor about getting married?

2) Some singles tend to put their life "on hold" until they get married. Have each member of your group describe something that he or she has been putting off until they get married.

3) Discuss what life would be like without a free will. Why must free will exist to enjoy true love?

4) In Matthew 22:30, Jesus states that there is no marriage in Heaven. Discuss why earthly marriage should not be the ultimate goal of a Christian.

Session #8 – Where's the Passion?
Realizing Your Role in Your Social Life

Kickoff Question:

If you lived in a culture of pre-arranged marriage, who would you trust more to select your spouse – your mother or your father? Why?

Video Introduction:

In the previous session, Rob explained two ways that God works on behalf of your social life. However, God has also given you a free will, because without free will, true love cannot exist. Therefore, you have a role to play in your relationships. In this final session, Rob discusses how your decisions directly affect the quality of your dating life.

Video Notes:

What Part do You Play in Your Social Life?

1. _____ to love the people you meet.

Marriage happens by _____ – not by chance.

2. Let go of the _____ to get married.

Why is Surrender so Important?

There is a difference between the desire for marriage and the

_____ for marriage.

Whenever you demand something from God, you _____

His love from benefiting that particular area of your life.

Whatever you depend upon for your happiness will always wind up

_____ you.

God does not promise you a _____.

> **Hebrews 13:21** – God will equip you in every good thing to do His will, working in you that which is pleasing in His sight, through Jesus Christ.

> **Psalm 37:4** – Delight yourself in the Lord, and He will give you the desires of your heart.

<u>Questions to consider:</u>

1. Am I dating to find someone to make me feel better about myself?

2. Am I content and thankful to God that I'm single right now?

3. Am I terrified of the possibility that I may never get married?

4. Is the love of Jesus Christ enough for me?

How does God want you to respond to what you heard today?

_____

_____

_____

_____

_____

For further study on the topics in this session, read Chapter 3
in Rob's book, *The Power of Passion*.

Personal Prayer
of Surrender

"Lord, I apologize for blaming my romantic frustrations on You. Thank You for creating marriage. However, if I never get married (or remarried), it is now okay with me.

As of today, Lord, I surrender my demand for marriage to You. Because, now I know that Your love will always complete me and fulfill my wildest dreams. Lord, help me to respond to the motivations you will place within me to love those who cross my path – with no strings attached.

May my relationships be avenues to express Your love through me to other people. You want the best for me, Lord, and I trust you to live Your life through me to build great relationships."

Signed: _____ Date: _____

Colossians 2:10 – ... and in Him you have been made complete...

Session #8
Small Group Discussion Questions

1) How can focusing on the needs of others help you become more attractive to date?

2) What is the difference between a desire for marriage and the demand for marriage? Why can the demand for marriage be a detriment to your life?

3) Read Hosea 2:16, 19-20. If God does not promise us earthly marriage, then what type of promise about marriage does He make?

4) After completing this study, what specific changes do you plan to make in the way you approach dating?

Notes:

Answers to fill-in-the-blank statements:

Session #1 – Discovering the Longing of Your Heart
Our society says the best way to satisfy your heart is through romantic passion.

A man wants to be loved as a hero. A woman feels loved when the hero wants her.

Why is relational heartache common among Christians? We try to fulfill our hearts with something that cannot satisfy.

The Problem with Romantic Passion:
Human love is like chocolate.
Romantic Passion is always temporary.
Romantic Passion is also always performance-based.
What we all want is to be unconditionally accepted.

Session #2 – Discovering Real Passion
The 3 Elements of Real Passion:
Element #1: Real Passion loves me initially.
Element #2: Real Passion loves me specifically.
Element #3: Real Passion loves me sacrificially.

Jesus Christ loves me: initially, specifically, and sacrificially.

Session #3 – Determining the Best Person to Date
Just because someone is attractive or professes to be a Christian does not make them a good marriage partner.

Pursue someone who attracts you specifically, but is willing to love you sacrificially.

As a Christian, you can trust your heart.

In Ephesians 5, God calls men to initiate a relationship.

Session #4 – Learning to Discern Character

Specific Attraction can bring two people together, but only <u>sacrifice</u> can keep them together.

The definition of Marriage is a <u>commitment</u> to an <u>imperfect</u> person for their <u>highest</u> good.

Character can only be determined over <u>time</u>.

Do not ask Jesus to give you more patience. Instead, ask Him to give you <u>His</u> patience.

Session #5 – Appreciating Sexual Desire

God primarily created sex to help you comprehend the <u>delight</u> that He feels for you.

If we use sex outside of marriage, then we destroy the <u>picture</u> that God intended it to be.

You were made to be <u>naked</u> and accepted.

Sex is a physical act that <u>superglues</u> the bodies and souls of two people together.

The Hidden Damage from Sexual Immorality:
1. Loss of the capacity to <u>feel</u> intimacy for another person.
2. Contraction of painful or deadly transmitted <u>diseases</u>.
3. Carrying a heavy, emotional <u>burden</u> of guilt and shame.

Session #6 – Resisting Sexual Temptation

Living by rules alone will encourage sin to <u>tempt</u> you.
How do you resist temptation? Let <u>Christ</u> fight the battle for you.

Healing Your Heart from a Sexual Mistake:
1. <u>Agree</u> with God that you misused His gift of sex.
2. <u>Forgive</u> yourself – knowing God has forgiven you.
3. Let you heart <u>heal</u> before you date again.

Session #7– Recognizing God's Role in Your Social Life
Marriage Myth #1: Marriage will make you <u>happy</u>.
Marriage Myth #2: If you're single, something must be <u>wrong</u> with you.

Is God to blame for singleness or social suffering? <u>No</u>
True love cannot exist without a <u>free</u> <u>will</u>.
The quality of your social life is based on the <u>choices</u> you make.

What Part does God Play in Your Social Life?
1. God promises to bring <u>people</u> across your <u>path</u>.
2. God promises to create <u>desires</u> within you to <u>love</u> those He brings across your path.

God does not intend to direct your love life through a bunch of extraordinary <u>signs</u>.

God's will for your social life is to <u>conform</u> your character into a loving kind of person.

Session #8– Realizing Your Role in Your Social Life
What Part do You Play in Your Social Life?
1. <u>Choose</u> to love the people you meet.
Marriage happens by <u>choice</u> – not by chance.
2. Let go of the <u>demand</u> to get married.

Why is Surrender so Important?
There is a difference between the desire for marriage and the <u>demand</u> for marriage.

Whenever you demand something from God, you <u>block</u> His love from benefiting that particular area of your life.

Whatever you depend upon for your happiness will always wind up <u>controlling</u> you.

God does not promise you a <u>spouse</u>.

Additional Power of Passion Resources

For small group study or Sunday School curriculum:

The Power of Passion
Applying the Love of Christ to Dating Relationships
8-session DVD Video Study
48-page Study Guide
Leaders Guide available

For personal study or devotions for dating couples:

The Power of Passion
Applying the Love of Christ to Dating Relationships
256-page softcover book by Rob Eagar
Discover how Christ's love answers the most common
dating issues that singles and young adults face.
Includes 24-page built-in Study Guide.

Events for churches and college campuses:

The Power of Passion Conference with Rob Eagar
A unique event where singles and young adults
enjoy a fun, relevant environment to build new
relationships and grow deeper with Christ.
To host an event or retreat, call 1-800-267-2045.

To order Power of Passion resources, contact:

Grace Press Publishing
3625 Chartwell Drive
Suwanee, GA 30024
1-800-267-2045
www.powerofpassion.com